P9-ARQ-143

# Raw food recipes made simple and easy

## Deliciously Quick Raw Food Recipes for Beginners

# Table of Contents

# Introduction

---

For many people, when they think of a satisfying meal they picture a steaming plate of food fresh from the oven. With this in mind, the concept of a raw food diet may seem strange to you at first but – after reading this book – you will realize that not only is it possible, it is entirely doable! A raw food diet may be just the thing you have been looking for to lose those stubborn pounds and to turn your life around completely.

But what is the draw of eating uncooked food? Why would anyone do it?

As more people turn to vegan and vegetarian lifestyles, raw foodism is gaining popularity as well. There is a great deal of evidence to support the health and benefits of this trend as more than just another fad diet. The raw food diet is a way of life and, once you try it, you may find it difficult to go back to anything else. In this book you will find all of the information you need to understand what the raw food diet is and how you can follow it yourself. But the benefits don't stop there – you will also receive a collection of tips and over 100 delicious recipes to get you started on your way.

# What is the Raw Food Diet?

---

The raw food diet is exactly what it sounds like – a diet consisting only of uncooked and unprocessed foods. The main components of the raw food diet include raw fruits, vegetables, seeds, nuts, sprouted grains, raw dairy products and some meat and seafood. Despite the name "raw food diet" – not everything you eat in this diet has to be completely uncooked. Foods can be heated up to 115°F (46°C) and still meet the requirements of the diet. Why can foods only be heated to 115°F? Raw foodists believe that the enzymes present in raw foods will be degraded or destroyed at temperatures above 120°F (49°C).

The raw food diet was first developed in Switzerland by medical doctor Maximilian Bircher-Benner. This doctor discovered the health benefits of raw food himself in recovering

12

from jaundice by eating raw apples. Following his recovery, Bircher-Benner conducted experiments regarding the effects of raw vegetables on human health. In 1897 he opened "Vital Force," a sanatorium which utilizes treatment plans based on logic determined by nature. Bircher-Benner's sanatorium is still treating patients today and his raw food diet is only becoming more popular as time passes.

Today, there are several different types of raw foodism: raw veganism, raw vegetarianism and raw animal food diets. Raw veganism is a diet which consists only of unprocessed plant foods and nothing is heated above 104°F (40°C). Within this category there are other subcategories including fruitarians, juicarians and sproutarians. Raw vegetarianism is somewhat less restricting than raw veganism because it allows for the consumption of raw dairy products and eggs. Raw animal food diets include all raw fruits, vegetables, nuts, seeds and sprouted grains along with raw dairy products and meats that can be eaten raw.

# Why Choose the Raw Food Diet?

If you have never heard of a raw food diet, it may seem like a foreign concept to you. Once you get used to it, however, you will find that it is not as strange as you may have thought. When you think about it, our ancestors would have followed a diet very similar to the raw food diet. Before the development of agriculture and modern technology, cooking methods were very simple and a majority of foods were eaten raw. Why should the type of diet you follow today be any different?

The raw food diet is more than just another fad diet based on counting calories and obsessing over every little thing you eat. Most of the foods included in the diet are naturally low in calories and high in nutrients, so you don't have to worry about whether something you eat will "ruin" your day. Many followers of vegan and vegetarian diets find that, after a few weeks of eating plant-based foods, they find that their sense of taste is enhanced – fruits and vegetables that may have once tasted bland are full of rich flavor, making each meal an experience.

If you are looking for a diet that is more than just a way to lose a couple pounds, the raw food diet may be the right choice for you. It is not just a trend, it is a lifestyle choice that will benefit you and your health in countless ways. In the next two sections you will learn the science behind the diet and just what some of those health benefits are.

# The Science Behind the Raw Food Diet

In order to truly understand why the raw food diet is a good choice you need to understand the science behind it. Why is it healthier to eat foods that haven't been heated above 115°F (46°C)? Does the raw food diet conform to modern dietary guidelines? What does the raw food diet have that other diets don't? Once you learn the answers to these questions you will be able to truly discern whether this is the right diet for you.

As you've already learned, the raw food diet has existed since the 1800s, though truly it is nothing new. Humans have eaten raw fruits and vegetables throughout their entire existence, so why should modern humans be any different? At this point you may see the merit of the raw food diet but you might still be looking for some scientific proof that it works. Countless studies and surveys have been conducted regarding the health and benefits of plant-based and raw diets and the statistics simply can't be denied.

A number of studies conducted between 1994 and 2004 support the conclusion that eating vegetables, both raw and cooked, results in a reduced risk for developing chronic disease like cancer. Other studies have forged a link between raw food consumption and reduced cholesterol levels, relief from the symptoms of rheumatoid arthritis and even improved mental health. The benefits of eating raw food are clear but what about the problems associated with eating cooked food?

Since the 1990s a number of studies have forged a link between the cooking of food and the production of harmful chemical compounds called heterocyclic amines (HCAs). High HCA rates have been linked to cancer in animal test subjects, though the link to cancer exposure in humans has yet to be confirmed. Studies have also shown that cooking foods and preserving them in salt leads to the formation of nitrosamines, a carcinogenic chemical compound which can be more accurately described as a toxin. Countless studies have shown that certain cooking methods and the cooking of certain foods leads to the formation of toxins which can have a serious impact on your health. Foods cooked below 115°F (46°C) and foods that are eaten raw generally do not have this problem.

# Health Benefits of the Diet

No matter which diet you choose, the benefits you experience might differ greatly from the benefits someone else experiences. Every person's body is different and every person's body reacts differently to the raw food diet. After reaching the last section, however, you should realize that the raw food diet holds the potential for some very real and very significant health benefits. You won't know until you try it yourself, however, what benefits are in store for you.

Some of the benefits associated with the raw food diet include:

- The diet is naturally low in calories which will support your weight loss efforts without you feeling starved or restricted

- The raw food diet is rich in nutrients which helps to reduce the risk of malnutrition and nutritional deficiencies

- The typical raw food diet is rich in fiber which helps to promote health digestion while reducing gastrointestinal issues such as gas and bloating

- Long-term consumption of plant-based foods has been shown to reduce cholesterol levels and to support heat health

- Studies have shown that increased consumption of raw vegetables may help to reduce the risk for certain types of cancer

- The enzymes present in uncooked foods are released into the mouth with chewing – these enzymes play a significant role in overall health and may be degraded or destroyed with cooking

- Studies have shown that participants in plant-based diets experience improved mental and emotional quality of life

- Several studies show that certain cooking methods create dangerous toxins like nitrosamines which have been linked to cancer and other serious diseases

- A study conducted by the Nutrition Society revealed that cooking may reduce the digestibility of certain foods

- Cooking foods requires either the direct or indirect use of energy and may contribute to the release of harmful gases which impact the environment

Now that you understand the science behind the raw food diet as well as some of the health benefits, you may be ready to make the switch. The following section includes a Quick-Start Guide to get you on your way toward a raw food diet and the following chapter will provide you with over 100 delicious recipes to get you started on the right foot.

# Quick-Start Guide

The raw food diet is an incredibly healthy option but it can be difficult to make the transition. In order to ensure that you are able to follow the diet for the long term, you need to make the transition slowly. Below you will find a collection of tips to help you get started in the raw food diet as well as pointers to make it easier to stick to the diet in the long run.

1. Understand that there are risks associated with eating raw food – if you clean all of your food properly, however, you shouldn't have to worry

2. Make the transition into a raw diet slowly – start by phasing out cooked foods over a period of 10 days or so, replacing it with raw foods

3. Don't be afraid to try out new flavors –
   take advantage of the spices in your spice
   rack and try plenty of different
   combinations to find what you like

4. Eat a variety of different foods – if you eat
   the same thing for every meal you are
   likely to get bored and will have trouble
   sticking to the diet

5. Don't be put off by claims that the raw
   food diet is too expensive – if you plan
   your meals and shop smart, any diet can
   be affordable

6. Eating out while on the raw food diet can
   be a challenge unless you plan ahead –
   look at menus online and find local
   restaurants that offer organic, vegan and
   vegetarian options

7. Take advantage of local farmers markets to find affordable, in-season produce for the raw food diet

8. Keep in mind that exercise is part of a healthy life and it can help you to meet your weight loss goals – incorporating moderate exercise into your routine will boost the results of your raw food diet

If your goal in switching to the raw food diet is to lose weight, keep in mind that the pounds will not melt off overnight. In fact, the more quickly you lose weight, the easier it will be to gain it back. The raw food diet is more than just a fad diet – it is a healthy lifestyle choice that will help you to meet your weight loss goals and improve your overall health.

# Delicious Raw Food Recipes

## Breakfast Recipes

---

## Maple Pecan Power Balls

---

**Prep Time**: 10 minutes

**Servings**: 2

**Ingredients**:

½ cup chopped pecans, divided

2 tbsp. shredded coconut, unsweetened

1 tbsp. raw maple syrup

2 tsp. coconut oil

1 tsp. water

¼ tsp. vanilla extract

Pinch ground cinnamon

**Directions**:

1. Set aside 1 to 2 tbsp. chopped pecans.
2. Place the remaining chopped pecans in a food processor and grind into a coarse flour.
3. Transfer the powdered nuts to a bowl and add the remaining ingredients, including the reserved chopped pecans.
4. Stir the mixture well, using your hands if needed to combine.
5. Shape the mixture into 1-inch balls by hand.
6. Chill the power balls for 1 hour until firm.

## Chocolate Coconut Power Balls

**Prep Time**: 10 minutes

**Servings**: 2

**Ingredients**:

½ cup chopped walnuts, divided

3 tbsp. shredded coconut, unsweetened

1 tbsp. raw honey

½ tbsp. raw cocoa powder

2 tsp. coconut oil

1 tsp. water

¼ tsp. coconut extract

Pinch ground cinnamon

**Directions**:

1. Set aside 1 to 2 tbsp. chopped walnuts.

2. Place the remaining chopped walnuts in a food processor and grind into a coarse flour.

3. Transfer the powdered nuts to a bowl and add the remaining ingredients, including the reserved chopped pecans.

4. Stir the mixture well, using your hands if needed to combine.

5. Shape the mixture into 1-inch balls by hand.

6. Chill the power balls for 1 hour until firm.

# Banana Walnut Pancakes

**Prep Time**:  1 hour

**Servings**:  2

**Ingredients**:

¾ cup ground flaxseed meal

¼ cup flax seeds

¼ cup unsweetened coconut, dried

1/3 cup water

2 tbsp. raw honey

2 tbsp. coconut butter

1 small banana, sliced

3 tbsp. finely chopped walnuts

**Directions**:

1. Combine all of the ingredients in a bowl and mix well by hand.

2. Shape the mixture into small patties.

3. Arrange the patties on a dehydrator shelf with a screen.

4. Dehydrate the pancakes for 30 minutes at 140°F then for another 30 minutes at 116°F.

## Blueberry Flaxseed Pancakes

---

**Prep Time**: 1 hour

**Servings**: 2

**Ingredients**:

¾ cup ground flaxseed meal

¼ cup flax seeds

¼ cup unsweetened coconut, dried

1/3 cup water

2 tbsp. raw honey

2 tbsp. coconut oil

½ cup fresh blueberries

**Directions**:

1. Combine all of the ingredients in a bowl and mix well by hand.
2. Shape the mixture into small patties.
3. Arrange the patties on a dehydrator shelf with a screen.

4. Dehydrate the pancakes for 30 minutes at 140°F then for another 30 minutes at 116°F.

## Chia Seed Breakfast Pudding

**Prep Time**: 30 minutes

**Servings**: 2

**Ingredients**:

1 cup water

¾ cup fresh orange juice

1/3 cup chia seeds

¼ cup almonds, soaked and drained

2 large pitted dates

Pinch ground cinnamon

**Directions**:

1. Combine the almonds and water in a blender and blend on high speed for 1 minute.
2. Strain the liquid through cheesecloth and discard the solids.

3. Place the liquid back in the blender with the dates and cinnamon then blend smooth.

4. Blend the orange juice into the liquid then pour into a bowl.

5. Stir in the chia seeds and let sit for 20 minutes.

6. Divide into two cups to serve.

## Quick and Easy Porridge

---

**Prep Time**: 5 minutes

**Servings**: 2

**Ingredients**:

1 ¼ cup water

½ cup chia seeds

2 tbsp. raisins

2 tbsp. shredded coconut, dried

1 tbsp. raw honey

1 tbsp. raw sunflower seeds

**Directions**:

1. Stir together the water and chia seeds in a bowl.

2. Add the remaining ingredients and stir well to serve.

# Chia Raisin Breakfast Pudding

**Prep Time**: 30 minutes

**Servings**: 2

**Ingredients**:

1 cup water

¾ cup fresh apple juice

1/3 cup chia seeds

¼ cup almonds, soaked and drained

¼ cup raisins, divided

Pinch ground cinnamon

**Directions**:

1. Combine the almonds and water in a blender and blend on high speed for 1 minute.
2. Strain the liquid through cheesecloth and discard the solids.

3. Place the liquid back in the blender with all but 1 tbsp. raisins and cinnamon then blend smooth.

4. Blend the apple juice into the liquid then pour into a bowl.

5. Stir in the chia seeds and let sit for 20 minutes.

6. Divide into two cups and top with remaining raisins to serve.

# Cinnamon Banana Crepes

**Prep Time**: 5 minutes

**Servings**: 2

**Ingredients**:

1 cup mashed banana

½ cup water

½ cup ground flaxseed meal

1 ½ tbsp. ground cinnamon

Pinch ground nutmeg

**Directions**:

1. Combine all of the ingredients in a blender on high speed until smooth.
2. Line your dehydrator tray with a nonstick liner.
3. Pour the batter into the dehydrator tray and dehydrate for 3 to 4 hours at 105°F.

4. Flip the partially finished crepe onto a mesh tray and remove the liner.

5. Use a sharp knife to score the crepes in the desired shapes.

6. Dehydrate for another 4 to 5 hours until dry but not crisp.

7. Remove from the dehydrator and fill with fresh fruit.

8. Roll the crepes up around the filling to serve.

# Pumpkin Flaxseed Crepes

**Prep Time**: 5 minutes

**Servings**: 2

**Ingredients**:

1 cup pumpkin puree

½ cup water

½ cup ground flaxseed meal

1 tbsp. ground cinnamon

1 tsp. ground nutmeg

**Directions**:

1. Combine all of the ingredients in a blender on high speed until smooth.
2. Line your dehydrator tray with a nonstick liner.
3. Pour the batter into the dehydrator tray and dehydrate for 3 to 4 hours at 105°F.

4. Flip the partially finished crepe onto a mesh tray and remove the liner.

5. Use a sharp knife to score the crepes in the desired shapes.

6. Dehydrate for another 4 to 5 hours until dry but not crisp.

7. Remove from the dehydrator and fill with fresh fruit.

8. Roll the crepes up around the filling to serve.

## Blueberry Banana Bowl

---

**Prep Time**: 5 minutes

**Servings**: 1

**Ingredients**:

2 small bananas, peeled and sliced

1 cup fresh blueberries

2 to 3 tbsp. unsweetened almond milk

Pinch ground cinnamon

**Directions**:

1. Combine the bananas and blueberries in a bowl and stir.
2. Add a splash of almond milk and sprinkle with cinnamon to serve.

## Raw Cinnamon Oatmeal

**Prep Time**: 10 minutes

**Servings**: 2

**Ingredients**:

1 ½ cups water

1 ¼ cup steel cut oats

1 apple, cored and chopped

2 tbsp. raisins

1 tsp. raw honey

½ tsp. ground cinnamon

**Directions**:

1. Combine the water, oats, raisins and honey into a blender and blend until smooth.

2. Add the apple and cinnamon then blend smooth to serve.

46

# Maple Walnut Oatmeal

---

**Prep Time**: 10 minutes

**Servings**: 2

**Ingredients**:

1 ½ cups water

1 ¼ cup steel cut oats

1 apple, cored and chopped

2 tbsp. chopped walnuts

1 tsp. raw maple syrup

½ tsp. ground cinnamon

**Directions**:

1. Combine the water, oats and maple syrup into a blender and blend until smooth.
2. Add the apple and cinnamon then blend smooth.
3. Top with chopped walnuts to serve.

# Fresh Raspberry Jam

**Prep Time**:  15 minutes

**Servings**:  3 to 4

**Ingredients**:

1 cup ripe raspberries

2 tbsp. chia seeds

**Directions**:

1.  Place the berries in a blender and blend until smooth.
2.  Pour the liquid into a bowl and stir in the chia seeds.
3.  Let sit for 5 to 10 minutes then stir before serving.

# Lemon Blackberry Jam

---

**Prep Time**: 15 minutes

**Servings**: 3 to 4

**Ingredients**:

1 cup ripe blackberries

2 tbsp. chia seeds

2 tbsp. fresh lemon juice

1 tsp. lemon zest

**Directions**:

1. Place the berries and lemon zest in a blender and blend until smooth.
2. Pour the liquid into a bowl and stir in the lemon juice and chia seeds.
3. Let sit for 5 to 10 minutes then stir before serving.

## Strawberry Jam

**Prep Time**: 15 minutes

**Servings**: 3 to 4

**Ingredients**:

1 cup fresh sliced strawberries

2 tbsp. chia seeds

**Directions**:

1. Place the berries in a blender and blend until smooth.
2. Pour the liquid into a bowl and stir in the chia seeds.
3. Let sit for 5 to 10 minutes then stir before serving.

## Bountiful Mixed Berry Salad

**Prep Time**:  5 minutes

**Servings**:  2

**Ingredients**:

1 ½ cups sliced strawberries

1 cup fresh blackberries

½ cup fresh blueberries

1 tbsp. fresh lime juice

**Directions**:

1. Combine all of the ingredients in a bowl and toss well.
2. Cover and chill until ready to serve.

## Tropical Fruit Salad

**Prep Time**:  5 minutes

**Servings**:  2

**Ingredients**:

1 ripe mango, pitted and chopped

1 cup chopped pineapple

1 navel orange, peeled and chopped

1 ripe kiwifruit, peeled and sliced

1 small banana, peeled and chopped

**Directions**:

1.  Combine all of the ingredients in a bowl and toss well.
2.  Cover and chill until ready to serve.

# Minty Mango Melon Salad

**Prep Time**:  5 minutes

**Servings**:  2

**Ingredients**:

1 cup chopped watermelon

1 cup chopped cantaloupe

1 cup chopped honeydew

½ ripe mango, pitted and chopped

1 tbsp. fresh lemon juice

3 tbsp. fresh chopped mint leaves

**Directions**:

1.  Combine all of the ingredients in a bowl and toss well.
2.  Cover and chill until ready to serve.

## Lunch Recipes

---

### Chopped Mango Avocado Salad

---

**Prep Time**: 5 minutes

**Servings**: 2

**Ingredients**:

1 ripe mango, pitted and chopped

½ ripe avocado, pitted and chopped

3 tbsp. fresh chopped cilantro

2 tbsp. diced red onion

1 tbsp. fresh chopped mint

1 tbsp. fresh lime juice

1 tbsp. fresh lemon juice

Pinch salt and pepper

**Directions**:

1. Combine all of the ingredients in a mixing bowl and toss to coat.

2. Chill until ready to serve.

## Strawberry Spinach Salad

**Prep Time**:  5 minutes

**Servings**:  2

**Ingredients**:

4 to 5 cups fresh baby spinach

1 cup diced fresh strawberries

¼ cup diced red onion

2 tbsp. diced celery

3 to 4 tbsp. preferred dressing

**Directions**:

1.  Combine the spinach, red onion and celery in a salad bowl.
2.  Toss well then top with diced strawberries.
3.  Chill until ready to serve and serve with preferred dressing.

# Walnut Apple Kale Salad

**Prep Time**:  5 minutes

**Servings**:  2

**Ingredients**:

3 cups chopped kale leaves

1 cup chopped romaine lettuce

1 medium carrot, grated

1 green onion, sliced

1 medium ripe apple, cored and chopped

3 tbsp. finely chopped walnuts

3 to 4 tbsp. preferred dressing

**Directions**:

1.  Combine the kale, lettuce, carrot and red onion in a salad bowl.
2.  Mix well then top with apple and sprinkle with walnuts.
3.  Serve with your preferred dressing.

## Chopped Broccoli Almond Salad

**Prep Time**: 5 minutes

**Servings**: 2

**Ingredients**:

2 ½ cups chopped broccoli

¼ cup diced red onion

¼ cup seedless raisins

2 tbsp. chopped almonds

2 tbsp. raw mayonnaise

2 tbsp. fresh lemon juice

1 tbsp. olive oil

1 tsp. raw honey

Pinch salt and pepper

**Directions**:

1. Combine the first four ingredients in a bowl and mix well.

2. Whisk together the remaining ingredients and toss with the salad to coat.

3. Chill until ready to serve.

## Summer Arugula Salad

**Prep Time**: 5 minutes

**Servings**: 2

**Ingredients**:

4 cups fresh arugula

2 green onions, sliced

½ cup thin-sliced seedless cucumber

¼ cup packed basil leaves, chopped

3 to 4 tbsp. preferred dressing

**Directions**:

1. Combine the arugula, green onion, cucumber and basil in a salad bowl.
2. Toss to combine and chill until ready to serve.

## Spinach and Grapefruit Salad

**Prep Time**:  5 minutes

**Servings**:  2

**Ingredients**:

4 cups fresh baby spinach

2 green onions, sliced thin

½ pink grapefruit, peeled and sectioned

¼ cup fresh parsley leaves, packed

3 to 4 tbsp. preferred dressing

**Directions**:

1.  Combine the spinach, green onion and parsley in a salad bowl.
2.  Toss well then top with sectioned grapefruit.
3.  Serve chilled with your preferred dressing.

## Minty Fruit Salad

**Prep Time**: 5 minutes

**Servings**: 2

**Ingredients**:

4 cups fresh spring greens

1 small apple, cored and chopped

¼ cup fresh raspberries

¼ cup fresh diced strawberries

¼ cup fresh mint leaves

2 tbsp. olive oil

1 tbsp. fresh lime juice

1 tsp. balsamic vinegar

1 tsp. raw honey

Pinch dry mustard powder

**Directions**:

1. Combine the greens, fruit and mint in a salad bowl and toss well.

2. Whisk together the remaining ingredients and pour over the salad.

3. Toss to coat then chill until ready to serve.

# Fresh Fennel Apple Salad

**Prep Time**: 5 minutes

**Servings**: 2

**Ingredients**:

2 bulbs fennel, sliced thin

1 medium apple, cut into matchsticks

¼ cup chopped walnuts

2 tbsp. olive oil

2 tbsp. fresh lemon juice

1 tbsp. raw honey

2 tsp. minced shallot

Pinch salt and pepper

**Directions**:

1. Combine the first three ingredients in a bowl and stir well.

2. Whisk together the remaining ingredients and pour over the salad.

3. Toss well to coat and chill until ready to serve.

# Lemon Balsamic Cucumber Salad

**Prep Time**:  5 minutes

**Servings**:  2

**Ingredients**:

2 medium English cucumbers, chopped

1 small carrot, grated

¼ small red onion, sliced thin

3 tbsp. fresh lemon juice

2 tsp. balsamic vinegar

1 tsp. raw honey

Pinch salt and pepper

**Directions**:

1.  Combine the cucumber, carrot and onion in a bowl and mix well.

2.  Whisk together the remaining ingredients and toss to coat.

3.  Chill until ready to serve.

## Honey Mustard Dressing

**Prep Time**: 5 minutes

**Servings**: 2

**Ingredients**:

2 tbsp. olive oil

2 tbsp. fresh lemon juice

1 tbsp. distilled white vinegar

1 tbsp. dry mustard powder

2 tsp. raw honey

Pinch salt

**Directions**:

1. Blend all the ingredients in a small bowl with a whisk until smooth.

## Basil Raspberry Vinaigrette

**Prep Time**: 5 minutes

**Servings**: 2

**Ingredients**:

2 tbsp. olive oil

1 tbsp. canola oil

1 tsp. raspberry vinegar

1 tsp. raw honey

1 tsp. dried basil

Pinch salt and pepper

**Directions**:

1. Blend all the ingredients in a small bowl with a whisk until smooth.

## Orange Tahini Dressing

**Prep Time**: 5 minutes

**Servings**: 2

**Ingredients**:

¼ cup raw tahini

¼ cup fresh orange juice

3 tbsp. nutritional yeast

2 tbsp. nama shoyu

1 tsp. minced garlic

**Directions**:

1. Blend all the ingredients in a small bowl with a whisk until smooth.

## Simple Italian Dressing

---

**Prep Time**:  5 minutes

**Servings**:  2

**Ingredients**:

2 tbsp. canola oil

1 tbsp. olive oil

2 ½ tsp. red wine vinegar

½ tsp. white wine vinegar

½ tsp. dried oregano

¼ tsp. dried basil

¼ tsp. dried parsley

Pinch salt and pepper

**Directions**:

1.  Blend all the ingredients in a small bowl with a whisk until smooth.

## Caesar Dressing

**Prep Time**: 5 minutes

**Servings**: 2

**Ingredients**:

¼ cup macadamia nuts

2 tbsp. pine nuts, soaked 4 hours

2 tbsp. coconut water

2 fresh basil leaves

2 tsp. fresh lemon juice

1 pitted date

Pinch salt and pepper

**Directions**:

1. Blend all the ingredients in blender until smooth.

## **Poppy Seed Dressing**

**Prep Time**:  5 minutes

**Servings**:  2

**Ingredients**:

2 tbsp. raw tahini

2 tbsp. fresh lime juice

1 tbsp. coconut water

2 tsp. raw honey

½ tbsp. poppy seeds

Pinch sea salt

**Directions**:

1.  Blend all the ingredients in a small bowl with a whisk until smooth.

# Vegan Ranch Dressing

**Prep Time**:  5 minutes

**Servings**:  2


**Ingredients**:


3 tbsp. chopped cashews, soaked 2 hours

2 tbsp. water

1 tbsp. apple cider vinegar

2 tsp. fresh chopped dill

2 tsp. fresh chopped parsley

1 tsp. fresh lemon juice

1 tsp. olive oil

Pinch salt

Pinch dried thyme

Pinch dried oregano

Pinch onion powder


**Directions**:

1. Blend all the ingredients in a small bowl with a whisk until smooth.

## Spicy Thai Dressing

**Prep Time**: 5 minutes

**Servings**: 2

**Ingredients**:

3 tbsp. water

2 tbsp. raw tahini

2 tbsp. melted coconut oil

3 tsp. nama shoyu

1 tsp. fresh lemon juice

½ tsp. dried coriander

Pinch cayenne pepper

**Directions**:

1. Blend all the ingredients in a small bowl with a whisk until smooth.

## Cream of Mushroom Soup

**Prep Time**:  10 minutes

**Servings**:  2

**Ingredients**:

1 ½ cups raw almond milk

1 ½ cups sliced mushrooms, assorted

¼ cup chopped onion

1 clove garlic, peeled

2 ½ tbsp. liquid aminos

Salt and pepper to taste

**Directions**:

1. Combine all of the ingredients in a blender.
2. Blend until smooth and well combined.
3. Chill until ready to serve.

## Spicy Tomato Gazpacho

**Prep Time**:  15 minutes

**Servings**:  2

**Ingredients**:

2 medium plum tomatoes, quartered

½ small English cucumber, quartered

½ small green pepper, chopped

2 tbsp. diced red onion

½ small jalapeno, seeded and minced

1 ½ cups organic tomato juice

1 tbsp. white wine vinegar

1 tbsp. olive oil

Salt and pepper to taste

**Directions**:

1.  Combine the vegetables in a food processor and pulse several times to finely chop – do not puree.

2.  Transfer the vegetables to a bowl and stir in the remaining ingredients.

3.  Cover and chill until ready to serve.

## Creamy Carrot Soup

**Prep Time**: 5 minutes

**Servings**: 2

**Ingredients**:

1 ½ cups chopped carrot

¾ cups water

¼ cup chopped hazelnuts

1 small apple, peeled and chopped

2 tsp. raw honey

½ tsp. ground cinnamon

½ tsp. ground ginger

Pinch salt and pepper

**Directions**:

1. Combine all of the ingredients in a blender.
2. Blend until smooth and well combined.
3. Chill until ready to serve.

79

# Watermelon Gazpacho

**Prep Time**: 15 minutes

**Servings**: 2

**Ingredients**:

1 cup fresh chopped watermelon

1 small tomato, diced

½ medium English cucumber, chopped

2 tbsp. olive oil

1 tbsp. minced red onion

1 tbsp. fresh chopped dill

Salt and pepper to taste

**Directions**:

1. Combine all of the ingredients in a blender.
2. Blend until smooth and well combined.
3. Chill until ready to serve.

## Chipotle Corn Soup

**Prep Time**: 10 minutes

**Servings**: 2

**Ingredients**:

6 ears fresh corn, kernels cut off

1 ½ cups water

¼ tsp. chipotle chili powder

Pinch paprika

Salt and pepper to taste

**Directions**:

1. Combine all of the ingredients in a blender.
2. Blend until smooth and well combined.
3. Chill until ready to serve.

## Tomato Avocado Soup

---

**Prep Time**: 5 minutes

**Servings**: 2

**Ingredients**:

1 ripe avocado, pitted and chopped

1 medium yellow onion, diced

1 small tomato, diced

½ red pepper, chopped

1 cup raw almond milk

2/3 cup water

1 clove garlic, minced

1 tsp. olive oil

Salt and pepper to taste

**Directions**:

1. Combine the avocado, onion, almond milk, water and garlic in a blender and blend until smooth.

2.  Transfer the mixture to a bowl and stir in the remaining ingredients.

3.  Chill until ready to serve.

# Pineapple Cucumber Gazpacho

**Prep Time**:  10 minutes

**Servings**:  2

**Ingredients**:

2 small English cucumbers, chopped

½ ripe pineapple, cored and chopped

½ cup fresh pineapple juice

1 ½ tbsp. olive oil

2 tsp. fresh lime juice

1 tsp. sea salt

Green onions to garnish

**Directions**:

1. Combine all of the ingredients in a blender.
2. Blend until smooth and well combined.
3. Chill until ready to serve and garnish with green onions.

## Red Pepper Soup

**Prep Time**:  5 minutes

**Servings**:  2

**Ingredients**:

2 cups chopped red pepper, divided

¾ cup water

1/3 cup raw cashews

Salt and pepper to taste

**Directions**:

1. Reserve ½ cup chopped peppers and set them aside.
2. Combine all of the remaining ingredients in a blender.
3. Blend until smooth and well combined.
4. Chill until ready to serve then pour into bowls and garnish with remaining red peppers.

## *Dinner Recipes*

---

### **Lemon Garlic Zucchini "Pasta"**

---

**Prep Time**:  10 minutes

**Servings**:  2

**Ingredients**:

1 large zucchini

1 tbsp. fresh lemon juice

2 tsp. minced garlic

2 tsp. olive oil

Salt and pepper to taste

**Directions**:

1.  Use a peeler to peel the zucchini into pasta-like strips.
2.  Set the zucchini aside in a bowl.

86

3. Add the remaining ingredients and toss well to coat.

## Veggie Burger on Greens

**Prep Time**:  10 minutes

**Servings**:  2

**Ingredients**:

1 cup chopped carrot

¾ cup chopped sweet potato

¾ cup chopped parsnip

½ ripe avocado, pitted and chopped

½ cup fresh chopped parsley

¼ cup chopped red onion

¼ cup fresh chopped dill

1 tsp. minced garlic

2 tbsp. tamari soy sauce

1 tsp. balsamic vinegar

1 tsp. olive oil

3 to 4 cups mixed leafy greens

**Directions**:

1. Combine the first three ingredients in a food processor and blend until smooth.
2. Transfer the mixture to paper towel and squeeze the water from it.
3. Place the mixture back in the food processor and add the remaining ingredients aside from the leafy greens.
4. Blend until smooth then shape into 4 patties by hand.
5. Serve the patties on a bed of leafy greens.

# Hummus Zucchini Pizza

**Prep Time**: 15 minutes

**Servings**: 2

**Ingredients**:

½ cup buckwheat

1/3 cup diced carrots

¼ cup walnuts, soaked and drained

2 tbsp. olive oil

½ tsp. dried Italian seasoning

2 to 3 tbsp. fresh hummus

1 small zucchini, sliced thin

**Directions**:

1. Soak the buckwheat in water overnight and rinse several times a day until the buckwheat is sprouted.
2. Combine the buckwheat and olive oil in a food processor and blend until smooth.

3. Add the remaining ingredients aside from the pesto and spinach and blend well.

4. Spread the mixture on a dehydrator sheet (non-stick) and dehydrate for 45 minutes at 140°F.

5. Reduce the heat to 115°F and dehydrate until the top of the crust is dry.

6. Spread the hummus on the pizza and top with zucchini slices to serve.

## Cilantro Mango Carrot Spring Rolls

**Prep Time**: 10 minutes

**Servings**: 2

**Ingredients**:

4 rice paper wrappers

1 ripe mango, pitted and sliced

2 medium carrots, grated

2 tbsp. fresh chopped cilantro

2 tbsp. fresh chopped chives

Salt and pepper to taste

**Directions**:

1. Dip the rice paper wrappers in lukewarm water for 20 seconds or so until they soften.

2. Lay the wraps out on a plate and divide the filling ingredients equally among them.

92

3. Roll the wraps up around the filling and cut in half to serve.

# Red Pepper Carrot "Pasta"

**Prep Time**:  10 minutes

**Servings**:  2

**Ingredients**:

6 large carrots, rinsed well

1 medium red pepper, chopped fine

2 tsp. olive oil

1 tsp. minced garlic

1 tbsp. tamari soy sauce

1 tbsp. nutritional yeast

1 tsp. raw honey

Salt and pepper to taste

**Directions**:

1.  Peel the carrot using a peeler to create pasta-like threads.

2.  Toss the carrot with the olive oil, garlic and red pepper.

94

3. Whisk together the remaining ingredients and toss with the "pasta" to coat.

## Tomato Basil Wraps

---

**Prep Time**: 10 minutes

**Servings**: 2

**Ingredients**:

4 leaves Boston lettuce

1 large plum tomato, chopped

¼ small red onion, sliced thin

3 tbsp. chopped fresh basil

1 tbsp. fresh lemon juice

2 tsp. olive oil

Salt and pepper to taste

**Directions**:

1. Lay the lettuce leaves out flat on a plate.
2. Arrange the chopped tomato down the center of each leaf.
3. Top the tomato with red onion and basil.

4. Whisk together the remaining ingredients and drizzle over the wraps.

## Easy Falafel Balls

---

**Prep Time**:  15 minutes

**Servings**:  2

**Ingredients**:

1 ¾ cups diced carrots

1 cup raw sunflower seeds

1 cup fresh chopped parsley

¼ cup ground flaxseed meal

2 tbsp. minced red onion

1 clove garlic, minced

½ tsp. ground cumin

½ tsp. curry powder

Pinch salt and pepper

**Directions**:

1. Blend the carrots in a food processor until finely pureed.
2. Add the remaining ingredients and pulse until well combined.
3. Roll the mixture into balls by hand and arrange them on dehydrator sheets.
4. Dehydrate for 2 to 12 hours on low heat until they reach the desired consistency.

## Spinach Pesto Pizza

---

**Prep Time**:  15 minutes

**Servings**:  2


**Ingredients**:

½ cup buckwheat

1/3 cup diced carrots

¼ cup walnuts, soaked and drained

2 tbsp. olive oil

½ tsp. dried Italian seasoning

2 to 3 tbsp. fresh pesto

2 cups chopped baby spinach


**Directions**:

1.  Soak the buckwheat in water overnight and rinse several times a day until the buckwheat is sprouted.

2.  Combine the buckwheat and olive oil in a food processor and blend until smooth.

3. Add the remaining ingredients aside from the pesto and spinach and blend well.

4. Spread the mixture on a dehydrator sheet (non-stick) and dehydrate for 45 minutes at 140°F.

5. Reduce the heat to 115°F and dehydrate until the top of the crust is dry.

6. Spread the pesto on the pizza and top with spinach to serve.

# Balsamic Zucchini "Pasta"

**Prep Time**:  10 minutes

**Servings**:  2

**Ingredients**:

1 large zucchini

2 tsp. olive oil

1 tsp. balsamic vinegar

½ tsp. raw honey

Salt and pepper to taste

**Directions**:

1. Use a peeler to peel the zucchini into pasta-like strips.
2. Set the zucchini aside in a bowl.
3. Add the remaining ingredients and toss well to coat.

## Mushroom Burgers

---

**Prep Time**: 15 minutes

**Servings**: 2

**Ingredients**:

1 cup chopped mushrooms, assorted

1 cup grated carrot

½ cup almond flour

1/3 cup minced red onion

3 tbsp. minced celery

½ cup ground walnuts, soaked and drained

2 tbsp. water

2 tbsp. tamari soy sauce

Salt and pepper to taste

**Directions**:

1. Combine the mushrooms, carrot, red onion and celery in a mixing bowl.

2. Add the walnuts and almond flour and stir well.

3. Whisk together the remaining ingredients then work into the mushroom mixture by hand.

4. Shape the mixture into patties.

5. Place the patties on a mesh dehydrator tray and cook for 1 hour at 140°F.

6. Cook the patties at 115°F for 3 to 4 hours then serve.

## Cilantro Avocado Wraps

**Prep Time**: 10 minutes

**Servings**: 2

**Ingredients**:

4 leaves Boston lettuce

1 medium carrot, cut into matchsticks

½ ripe avocado, pitted and sliced

¼ small red onion, sliced thin

3 tbsp. chopped cilantro leaves

1 tbsp. fresh lemon juice

2 tsp. olive oil

Salt and pepper to taste

**Directions**:

1. Lay the lettuce leaves out flat on a plate.
2. Arrange the sliced avocado down the center of each leaf.

3. Top the avocado with carrot, red onion and cilantro.

4. Whisk together the remaining ingredients and drizzle over the wraps.

## Nut-Free Pizza Crust

**Prep Time**:

**Servings**:  2

**Ingredients**:

1/3 cup chia seeds

Water as needed

2 cups chopped spinach

1 small sweet potato

¼ cup fresh oregano

¼ cup fresh basil leaves, chopped

Salt and pepper to taste

**Directions**:

1. Place the chia seeds in a glass jar and cover with water.

2. Cover the jar and refrigerate for several hours.

3. Pulse the sweet potato in a food processor until nearly pureed.

4. Add the remaining ingredients and blend well.

5. Add in the soaked chia seeds and blend until a wet dough forms.

6. Spread the dough on a lined dehydrator sheet and dehydrate at 115°F for several hours until crisp.

## Carrot "Pasta" with Red Onion

**Prep Time**: 10 minutes

**Servings**: 2

**Ingredients**:

6 large carrots, rinsed well

1 small red onion, sliced thin

2 tsp. olive oil

1 tsp. minced garlic

1 tsp. minced ginger

1 tbsp. tamari soy sauce

1 tbsp. nutritional yeast

1 tsp. raw honey

Salt and pepper to taste

**Directions**:

1. Peel the carrot using a peeler to create pasta-like threads.

2. Toss the carrot with the olive oil, garlic and red onion.

3. Whisk together the remaining ingredients and toss with the "pasta" to coat.

# Mango Avocado Spring Rolls

**Prep Time**:  10 minutes

**Servings**:  2

**Ingredients**:

4 rice paper wrappers

½ ripe mango, pitted and sliced

½ ripe avocado, pitted and sliced

2 medium carrots, grated

2 tbsp. fresh chopped chives

1 tbsp. fresh chopped cilantro

1 tbsp. fresh chopped basil

Salt and pepper to taste

**Directions**:

1.  Dip the rice paper wrappers in lukewarm water for 20 seconds or so until they soften.

2. Lay the wraps out on a plate and divide the filling ingredients equally among them.

3. Roll the wraps up around the filling and cut in half to serve.

## Snacks and Beverages

---

### Cinnamon Banana Chips

---

**Prep Time**: 5 minutes

**Servings**: 2

**Ingredients**:

3 to 4 large bananas, sliced thin

Lemon juice as needed

Ground cinnamon to taste

**Directions**:

1. Place the bananas in a bowl and toss with lemon juice and ground cinnamon.

2. Arrange the slices on a dehydrator sheet and dry at 118°F and 10 to 12 hours until dry.

113

## Ginger Kale Chips

**Prep Time**: 5 minutes

**Servings**: 2

**Ingredients**:

2 bunches fresh kale, rinsed well

3 tbsp. olive oil

1 tsp. sea salt

Ground ginger to taste

**Directions**:

1. Break the kale into chunks by hand.
2. Whisk together the olive oil, ginger and salt in a large bowl.
3. Add the kale to the bowl and toss well to coat.
4. Spread the kale on dehydrator sheets and dry at 115°F for 4 to 6 hours or until the chips are crisp.

## Lime Coconut Macaroons

**Prep Time**: 15 minutes

**Servings**: 6

**Ingredients**:

1 cup shredded unsweetened coconut

1/3 cup blanched almond flour

2 tbsp. raw agave nectar

1 tbsp. fresh lime juice

1 tbsp. fresh lime zest

Pinch salt

**Directions**:

1. Combine the almond flour, lime juice, lime zest and salt in a food processor and blend well.

2. Add the remaining ingredients and pulse until the mixture starts to stick together.

3. Shape the mixture into 6 balls by hand and arrange on a dehydrator sheet.

4. Dehydrate for 12 hours on low heat until dried but still chewy.

## Grain-Free Crackers

**Prep Time**:

**Servings**:  2 to 30 minutes

**Ingredients**:

1 ¼ cup water, divided

½ cup flax seeds

½ cup raw oat flour

2 tbsp. sesame seeds

1 tbsp. dried onion

Salt and pepper to taste

**Directions**:

1.  Soak the flax seeds in 1 cup water for about 5 hours then drain.
2.  Combine the soaked flax seeds with the oat flour, remaining water, dried onion, salt and pepper in a mixing bowl.

117

3. Spread the mixture onto dehydrator sheet about ¼-inch thick.

4. Sprinkle with sesame seeds and score the crackers in the desired shape with a knife.

5. Dehydrate at 140°F for 30 minutes then reduce heat and dry at 115°F for 2 hours.

6. Transfer the crackers to mesh screen dehydrator sheets and dry for 2 to 4 more hours.

# Chipotle Zucchini Chips

**Prep Time**: 5 minutes

**Servings**: 2

**Ingredients**:

2 large zucchini, rinsed

3 tbsp. olive oil

1 tsp. sea salt

Chipotle seasoning to taste

**Directions**:

1. Slice the zucchini as thin as possible.
2. Whisk together the olive oil and salt in a large bowl.
3. Add zucchini to the bowl and toss well to coat.
4. Spread the kale on dehydrator sheets and sprinkle with seasoning.

5. Dry at 115°F for 4 to 6 hours or until the chips are crisp.

## Easy Apple Chips

**Prep Time**:  5 minutes

**Servings**:  2

**Ingredients**:

4 medium apples, cored and sliced thin

Lemon juice as needed

Ground cinnamon to taste

**Directions**:

1.  Place the apples in a bowl and toss with lemon juice and ground cinnamon.
2.  Arrange the slices on a dehydrator sheet and dry at 118°F and 10 to 12 hours until dry.

## Chia Seed Crackers

**Prep Time**:

**Servings**:


**Ingredients**:


¾ cups chia seeds

2 small bulbs fennel

2 medium apples

1 medium ripe tomato

2 tbsp. fresh lemon juice

2 cloves garlic, minced

Salt and pepper to taste


**Directions**:


1. Run the fennel, apples and tomato through a juicer.
2. Transfer the juice to a blender and add the lemon juice, garlic, salt and pepper.
3. Blend well then pour into a bowl.

4.  Stir in the chia seeds then let sit for 30 minutes.

5.  Spread the mixture as thinly as possible onto non-stick dehydrator sheets.

6.  Dry at 115°F for 4 hours then remove to a cutting board.

7.  Cut the crackers into the desired shape then place back in dehydrator sheets and dry for another 12 to 14 hours at 115°F.

# Lemon Honey Coconut Macaroons

**Prep Time**:  15 minutes

**Servings**:  6


**Ingredients**:


1 cup shredded unsweetened coconut

1/3 cup blanched almond flour

2 tbsp. raw honey

1 tbsp. fresh lemon juice

1 tbsp. fresh lemon zest

Pinch salt


**Directions**:


1.  Combine the almond flour, lemon juice, lemon zest and salt in a food processor and blend well.

2.  Add the remaining ingredients and pulse until the mixture starts to stick together.

3. Shape the mixture into 6 balls by hand and arrange on a dehydrator sheet.

4. Dehydrate for 12 hours on low heat until dried but still chewy.

## Lemon Zucchini Chips

**Prep Time**:  5 minutes

**Servings**:  2

**Ingredients**:

2 large zucchini, rinsed

2 tbsp. lemon juice

1 tbsp. olive oil

1 tsp. sea salt

**Directions**:

1. Slice the zucchini as thin as possible.
2. Whisk together the lemon juice, olive oil and salt in a large bowl.
3. Add zucchini to the bowl and toss well to coat.
4. Spread the kale on dehydrator sheets.
5. Dry at 115°F for 4 to 6 hours or until the chips are crisp.

126

# Ginger Apple Carrot Juice

**Prep Time**: 5 minutes

**Servings**: 2

**Ingredients**:

4 medium carrots

2 medium ripe apples

½ bunch fresh parsley

1 inch fresh gingerroot

½ lemon, peeled

**Directions**:

1. Feed the ingredients through your juicer in the order listed.

2. Stir the juice and divide between two cups.

3. Drink the juice immediately for the best flavor.

# Raspberry Coconut Smoothie

**Prep Time**: 5 minutes

**Servings**: 2

**Ingredients**:

1 ½ cups frozen raspberries

1 cup coconut water

¼ cup shredded unsweetened coconut

1 tsp. coconut oil

1 tsp. raw honey

½ tsp. coconut extract

**Directions**:

1. Combine the ingredients in a blender and blend until smooth.
2. Pour into two glasses and drink immediately.

# Savory Spring Greens Juice

**Prep Time**: 5 minutes

**Servings**: 2

**Ingredients**:

2 large leaves curly kale

2 large leaves romaine lettuce

1 handful fresh cilantro

1 handful fresh basil

1 handful fresh parsley

1 medium ripe apple

½ lemon, peeled

1 clove garlic, peeled

Pinch ground cinnamon

**Directions**:

1. Feed the ingredients through your juicer in the order listed.

2. Stir the juice and divide between two cups.

3. Drink the juice immediately for the best flavor.

# Blueberry Collard Green Smoothie

**Prep Time**: 5 minutes

**Servings**: 2

**Ingredients**:

2 cups chopped collard greens

1 cup frozen blueberries

½ cup water

½ cup organic apple juice

1 tsp. raw honey

**Directions**:

1. Combine the ingredients in a blender and blend until smooth.

2. Pour into two glasses and drink immediately.

## Spicy Celery Cucumber Juice

**Prep Time**: 5 minutes

**Servings**: 2

**Ingredients**:

3 large stalks celery

1 large English cucumber, quartered

1 medium carrot

1 medium ripe apple

½ jalapeno, seeded

Pinch cayenne pepper

**Directions**:

1. Feed the ingredients through your juicer in the order listed.
2. Stir the juice and divide between two cups.
3. Drink the juice immediately for the best flavor.

## Tropical Mango Smoothie

**Prep Time**: 5 minutes

**Servings**: 2

**Ingredients**:

2 cups frozen chopped mango

1 cup homemade almond milk

½ frozen banana, sliced

1 tsp. raw honey

**Directions**:

1. Combine the ingredients in a blender and blend until smooth.

2. Pour into two glasses and drink immediately.

# Watermelon Mango Juice

**Prep Time**: 5 minutes

**Servings**: 2

**Ingredients**:

2 cups chopped watermelon

2 large stalks celery

1 ripe mango, pitted

1 medium carrot

½ fresh lemon, peeled

**Directions**:

1. Feed the ingredients through your juicer in the order listed.
2. Stir the juice and divide between two cups.
3. Drink the juice immediately for the best flavor.

# Kale Cucumber Smoothie

---

**Prep Time**:  5 minutes

**Servings**:  2

**Ingredients**:

1 cup chopped kale leaves

1 cup water

½ medium English cucumber

½ cup organic apple juice

1 tbsp. fresh lemon juice

1 tsp. stevia powder

Dash cinnamon

**Directions**:

1. Combine the ingredients in a blender and blend until smooth.
2. Pour into two glasses and drink immediately.

## *Side Dish Recipes*

---

## Kale, Avocado and Sprout Salad

---

**Prep Time**: 5 minutes

**Servings**: 2

**Ingredients**:

1 cup pea shoots or sprouts

1 ripe avocado, pitted and diced

½ bunch kale leaves, de-stemmed and chopped

1 tbsp. fresh lemon juice

1 tbsp. fresh lime juice

Pinch salt and pepper

**Directions**:

1. Combine the pea shoots, avocado and kale in a bowl.

2. Add the remaining ingredients and toss well to coat.

## Balsamic Marinated Onions

**Prep Time**: 5 minutes

**Servings**: 2

**Ingredients**:

1 lbs. yellow onions, sliced

¼ cup olive oil

¼ cup balsamic vinegar

**Directions**:

1. Place the onions in a bowl.
2. Whisk together the remaining ingredients and pour over the onions.
3. Toss to coat and chill for 24 hours to marinade.
4. Drain the extra marinade before serving.

## Tomato Basil Spread

**Prep Time**: 5 minutes

**Servings**: 2 to 3

**Ingredients**:

1 cup soaked cashews

¼ cup soaked walnuts

¼ cup water

2 tbsp. chopped basil leaves

1 tbsp. olive oil

1 clove garlic, minced

Pinch salt and pepper

1 cup diced tomatoes

**Directions**:

1. Combine all of the ingredients in a food processor and blend until smooth.
2. Add the tomatoes and pulse until well combined.

## Raw Dill Sauerkraut

---

**Prep Time**: 5 minutes

**Servings**: 2

**Ingredients**:

½ head green cabbage, shredded

½ tbsp. dried dill

½ tbsp. caraway seeds

Salt and pepper to taste

**Directions**:

1. Chop the cabbage as desired and place it in a bowl.

2. Sprinkle the salt over the cabbage and massage it through.

3. Let the cabbage sit for 10 minutes then repeat the processes as needed until most of the liquid has been extracted.

4. Stir in the caraway seeds and dill then transfer the cabbage to a jar.

5. Seal the lid then store the jar in a cool dark place to ferment for 3 to 4 days.

6. Once opened, store in the refrigerator.

## **Almond Raisin Quinoa**

**Prep Time**:  10 minutes

**Servings**:  2

**Ingredients**:

1 cup sprouted quinoa

½ cup seedless raisins

2 tbsp. chia seeds

¼ cup chopped almonds

2 tbsp. fresh lemon juice

2 tbsp. olive oil

1 tbsp. raw honey

Pinch salt and pepper

**Directions**:

1.  Combine the quinoa, raisins, chia seeds and almonds in a bowl.

2.  Whisk together the remaining ingredients and pour over the quinoa mixture.

142

3. Toss well to coat and serve immediately.

# Lemon Balsamic Marinated Carrots

**Prep Time**:  5 minutes

**Servings**:  2

**Ingredients**:

1 lbs. carrots, sliced thin

¼ cup olive oil

¼ cup balsamic vinegar

Pinch salt and pepper

**Directions**:

1. Place the carrots in a bowl.
2. Whisk together the remaining ingredients and pour over the carrots.
3. Toss to coat and chill for 24 hours to marinade.
4. Drain the extra marinade before serving.

# Cashew "Cheese" Spread

**Prep Time**: 5 minutes

**Servings**: 2 to 3

**Ingredients**:

½ cup soaked cashews

¼ cup sundried tomatoes in oil, chopped

1 clove garlic, minced

1 tbsp. minced shallot

1 tsp. fresh lemon juice

Salt and pepper to taste

**Directions**:

1. Combine all of the ingredients in a food processor and blend until smooth.

## Easy Olive Tapenade

**Prep Time**: 5 minutes

**Servings**: 2

**Ingredients**:

1/3 cup pitted black olives

¼ cup pitted green olives

1 ½ tbsp. olive oil

1 clove garlic, minced

2 tsp. fresh chopped thyme

½ tsp. dried rosemary

**Directions**:

1. Combine all of the ingredients in a food processor and pulse until finely chopped.
2. Chill until ready to serve.

## Carrot Celery Salad

**Prep Time**: 5 minutes

**Servings**: 2

**Ingredients**:

¼ cup raw cashews

1 ½ tbsp. water

½ tsp. minced garlic

Pinch salt and pepper

1 cup grated carrot

¼ cup diced celery

2 tbsp. minced red onion

1 tbsp. chopped parsley

**Directions**:

1. Combine the first four ingredients in a food processor and blend until smooth.

2. In another bowl, stir together the carrot, celery, red onion and parsley.

3. Add the cashew mixture and toss to coat.

4. Chill until ready to serve.

## *Dessert Recipes*

---

## **Cinnamon Stuffed Apples**

**Prep Time**: 5 minutes

**Servings**: 2

**Ingredients**:

2 medium ripe apples

½ cup raw almonds

2 tsp. raw honey

1 tsp. ground cinnamon

**Directions**:

1. Combine the almond and cinnamon in a food processor and blend until a fine powder forms.

2. Core the apples and use a melon baller to scoop out most of the pulp.

3. Transfer the almond mixture to a bowl and add the apple pulp and raw honey.

4. Mix well then spoon back into the apples to serve.

# Frozen Lemon Raspberry Dessert

**Prep Time**: 5 minutes

**Servings**: 2

**Ingredients**:

2 medium frozen bananas, sliced

½ cup frozen raspberries

1 ½ tbsp. raw honey

1 ½ tbsp. fresh lemon juice

**Directions**:

1. Combine all of the ingredients in a food processor.

2. Pulse two or three times to chop the frozen banana.

3. Blend until smooth then spoon into dessert cups to serve.

# Frozen Chocolate Banana Dessert

**Prep Time**:  5 minutes

**Servings**:  2

**Ingredients**:

3 medium frozen bananas, sliced

1 ½ tbsp. raw honey

2 tsp. raw cocoa

**Directions**:

1. Combine all of the ingredients in a food processor.
2. Pulse two or three times to chop the frozen banana.
3. Blend until smooth then spoon into dessert cups to serve.

# Frozen Strawberry Dessert

**Prep Time**: 5 minutes

**Servings**: 2

**Ingredients**:

2 medium frozen bananas, sliced

1 cup frozen sliced strawberries

1 tbsp. raw honey

**Directions**:

1. Combine all of the ingredients in a food processor.

2. Pulse two or three times to chop the frozen banana.

3. Blend until smooth then spoon into dessert cups to serve.

## Cashew Cream

---

**Prep Time**:  5 minutes

**Servings**:  2

**Ingredients**:

½ cup raw cashews

½ cup water

1 small ripe apple, cored and chopped

2 tsp. raw honey

**Directions**:

1. Blend the cashews in a food processor until a fine powder forms.
2. Add the water and blend smooth.
3. Add the remaining ingredients and blend until well combined.

# Whipped Coconut Cream

**Prep Time**: 5 minutes

**Servings**: 6 to 8

**Ingredients**:

1 can full-fat coconut milk

½ tsp. stevia powder

½ tsp. vanilla extract

**Directions**:

1. Refrigerate the coconut milk upside down overnight.
2. Flip the can right-side up and open it.
3. Pour the liquid into a bowl and set aside for another recipe.
4. Spoon the coconut into a bowl and add the stevia and vanilla extract.
5. Whip the coconut on high speed until light and fluffy.

## Coconut Fudge

**Prep Time**: 10 minutes

**Servings**: 2 to 3

**Ingredients**:

3 tbsp. almond butter

3 tbsp. unsweetened shredded coconut

1 ½ tbsp. raw cocoa powder

1 tbsp. raw honey

**Directions**:

1. Combine the ingredients in a food processor and pulse until it starts to stick together.
2. Shape the mixture into a square on a parchment-lined baking sheet and chill until set.

## Chocolate Walnut Fudge

**Prep Time**:  10 minutes

**Servings**:  2 to 3

**Ingredients**:

3 tbsp. almond butter

2 tbsp. chopped walnuts

1 ½ tbsp. raw cocoa powder

1 tbsp. raw honey

**Directions**:

1.  Combine the ingredients in a food processor and pulse until it starts to stick together.

2.  Shape the mixture into a square on a parchment-lined baking sheet and chill until set.

## **Blueberry Coconut Pie**

---

**Prep Time**:  15 minutes

**Servings**:  6

**Ingredients**:

2 ½ cups chopped walnuts

1 ¼ cup shredded unsweetened coconut

½ cup fresh lime juice

8 large pitted dates

1 ripe kiwi, peeled and sliced

1 tbsp. raw honey

2 to 3 cups fresh blueberries

**Directions**:

1.  In two different bowls, soak the walnuts and dates in water overnight.

2.  Drain the walnuts and dates and place them in a food processor and blend until well combined.

158

3. Add the kiwi, honey, coconut and lime juice and blend until smooth.

4. Press the mixture into the bottom of a pie plate and top with fresh blueberries to serve.

## Strawberry Lemon Pie

---

**Prep Time**:  15 minutes

**Servings**:  6

**Ingredients**:

2 ½ cups chopped walnuts

1 ¼ cup shredded unsweetened coconut

1 ripe kiwi, peeled and sliced

½ cup fresh lemon juice

8 large pitted dates

1 tbsp. raw agave nectar

2 ½ cups fresh sliced strawberries

**Directions**:

1.  In two different bowls, soak the walnuts and dates in water overnight.

2.  Drain the walnuts and dates and place them in a food processor and blend until well combined.

160

3. Add the kiwi, agave, coconut and lemon juice and blend until smooth.

4. Press the mixture into the bottom of a pie plate and top with fresh strawberries to serve.

## Chocolate Raspberry Pie

---

**Prep Time**:  15 minutes

**Servings**:  6

**Ingredients**:

2 ½ cups chopped walnuts

1 ¼ cup shredded unsweetened coconut

½ cup fresh lemon juice

8 large pitted dates

1 ripe kiwi, peeled and sliced

1 tbsp. raw honey

1 ½ tbsp. raw cocoa, divided

2 to 3 cups fresh raspberries

**Directions**:

1. In two different bowls, soak the walnuts and dates in water overnight.
2. Drain the walnuts and dates and place them in a food processor and blend until well combined.
3. Add the kiwi, honey, coconut, lemon juice and 1 tbsp. raw cocoa then blend until smooth.
4. Press the mixture into the bottom of a pie plate.
5. Toss the raspberries with the remaining cocoa and arrange in the pie crust to serve.

## Honey Walnut Cookies

---

**Prep Time**: 10 minutes

**Servings**: 2 dozen

**Ingredients**:

2 cups raw cashews, soaked in water 6 hours

1 cup unsweetened shredded coconut

¾ cup water

½ cup raw honey

½ cup chopped pecans

**Directions**:

1. Combine the first four ingredients in a food processor and blend smooth.
2. Fold the chopped nuts by hand.
3. Drop the batter in heaping teaspoons onto a non-stick dehydrator sheet.
4. Dehydrate for 30 minutes at 140°F and dry for 6 hours at 115°F.

164

5. Transfer the cookies to mesh dehydrator screens and continue drying for 4 to 6 more hours.

## Chocolate Chip Cookies

**Prep Time**: 15 minutes

**Servings**: 2 dozen

**Ingredients**:

2 cups raw cashews, soaked in water 6 hours

1 cup unsweetened shredded coconut

¾ cup water

½ cup raw agave nectar

½ cup raw cocoa nibs

**Directions**:

1. Combine the first four ingredients in a food processor and blend smooth.
2. Fold the raw cocoa nibs by hand.
3. Drop the batter in heaping teaspoons onto a non-stick dehydrator sheet.
4. Dehydrate for 30 minutes at 140°F and dry for 6 hours at 115°F.

5. Transfer the cookies to mesh dehydrator screens and continue drying for 4 to 6 more hours.

## **Maple Cashew Cookies**

---

**Prep Time**:  15 minutes

**Servings**:  2 dozen

**Ingredients**:

2 cups raw cashews, soaked in water 6 hours

1 cup unsweetened shredded coconut

¾ cup water

½ cup raw maple syrup

**Directions**:

1.  Combine all of the ingredients in a food processor and blend smooth.
2.  Fold the chopped nuts by hand.
3.  Drop the batter in heaping teaspoons onto a non-stick dehydrator sheet.
4.  Dehydrate for 30 minutes at 140°F and dry for 6 hours at 115°F.

5. Transfer the cookies to mesh dehydrator screens and continue drying for 4 to 6 more hours.

## Strawberry Kiwi Sorbet

**Prep Time**: 5 minutes

**Servings**: 2

**Ingredients**:

1 cup frozen strawberries, sliced

4 ripe medium kiwi, peeled and sliced

1/4 cup water

1 tbsp. raw honey

**Directions**:

1. Combine all of the ingredients in a blender and blend until smooth.
2. Pour the mixture into an ice cream maker and freeze according to the manufacturer's directions.

## Cranberry Banana Sorbet

---

**Prep Time**: 5 minutes

**Servings**: 2 to 3

**Ingredients**:

1 medium frozen banana, sliced

½ cup fresh cranberries

½ cup frozen peach slices

¼ cup frozen strawberries

2 tsp. raw honey

**Directions**:

1. Combine all of the ingredients in a blender and blend until smooth.

## Triple Berry Sorbet

---

**Prep Time**: 5 minutes

**Servings**: 2 to 3

**Ingredients**:

1 cup frozen strawberries

1/3 cup frozen raspberries

1/3 cup frozen blueberries

1/3 cup water

2 tbsp. fresh lemon juice

1 tbsp. raw honey

1 tsp. melted coconut oil

**Directions**:

1. Combine all of the ingredients in a blender and blend until smooth.

2. Pour the mixture into an ice cream maker and freeze according to the manufacturer's directions.

# Almond Chai Pudding

**Prep Time**: 10 minutes

**Servings**: 2

**Ingredients**:

1 ½ cup coconut water

3 tbsp. chia seeds

3 tbsp. raw almond butter

¼ tsp. ground cinnamon

Pinch vanilla powder

**Directions**:

1. Combine all of the ingredients in a blender and blend until smooth.

2. Let sit for 5 minutes to thicken before serving.

## Easy Vanilla Pudding

**Prep Time**:  10 minutes

**Servings**:  2

**Ingredients**:

1 ¼ cup unsweetened almond milk

3 tbsp. chia seeds

2 tsp. vanilla extract

**Directions**:

1.  Combine all of the ingredients in a blender and blend until smooth.
2.  Let sit for 5 minutes to thicken before serving.

# Chia Pumpkin Pudding

**Prep Time**:  10 minutes

**Servings**:  2 to 3

**Ingredients**:

½ cup pumpkin puree

½ unsweetened almond milk

2 tbsp. raw honey

1 ½ tbsp. chia seeds

¼ tsp. stevia powder

Pinch cinnamon and nutmeg

**Directions**:

1.  Combine all of the ingredients in a blender and blend until smooth.

2.  Let sit for 5 minutes to thicken before serving.

# Conclusion

Hopefully, after reading this book, you have a better understanding of what the raw food diet is. With that understanding you should be able to make an informed decision regarding whether it is the right diet for you. The raw food diet may take some getting used to, especially if you are used to eating a meat-and-potatoes type of diet. Once you get started, however, you will experience a wealth of new flavors and a variety of health benefits that will convince you to never go back. So what are you waiting for? The sooner you get started, the sooner you will reach your health and weight loss goals!

**Enjoy the recipes included in this book and good luck to you as you get started on your way in the raw food diet!**

Made in the USA
Lexington, KY
22 January 2018